T0128472

Poetry to Meditate On

KARON SCHLICKER

WESTBOW
PRESS®
A DIVISION OF THOMAS NELSON
& ZONDERVAN

Scripture taken from the New King James Version®. Copyright © 1982 by Thomas Nelson. Used by permission. All rights reserved.

WestBow Press books may be ordered through booksellers or by contacting:

WestBow Press
A Division of Thomas Nelson & Zondervan
1663 Liberty Drive
Bloomington, IN 47403
www.westbowpress.com
1 (866) 928-1240

ISBN: 978-1-9736-4613-6 (sc)
ISBN: 978-1-9736-4614-3 (e)

Library of Congress Control Number: 2018913810

Print information available on the last page.

WestBow Press rev. date: 12/06/2018

Foreword

When I first met Karon, I immediately knew she was a person of God who treated everyone with kindness. Her past and present experiences give her strength and knowledge for a greater understanding of faith and what it takes to live with faith. From the loss of her husband and sister to her amusing and heartfelt life with her great-nephew, she has grown to be more understanding of life and of the importance of one's relationships with the people in one's life.

I've known Karon for almost two years now. She has been writing poetry, daily, for over thirty-five years. Her writings include her perspective and experience on family, love, and loss, as well as her devotion to God and how He guides her through life. Her passionate outlook on life's experiences and her advice regarding what to do to overcome the difficult experiences is why you would enjoy *Poetry to Meditate On*.

Allison Pheasant

Preface

Since my last book, even more people have encouraged me to publish what I have written. I have been writing poetry for thirty-seven years. It helps me keep in touch with God and gives me courage to get on with my work in Him. I pray that these poems bless you as they have blessed me in writing them.

Introduction

These poems are written by the inspiration of God for spiritual growth and encouragement.

Grain of Mustard Seed

Father, I need to change my habits that
are not a reflection of You.
But You said if I had faith as small as the grain of
a mustard seed, this You would help me do.

When the weakness sets in and I cling to that seed,
I count on Your promises to help me weed out the weeds.

I know I am weak, ever so weak!
And I'm sure that when I feel this way,
it's just Your name I must speak.

A mustard seed is just a small thing that grows into a giant.
With that seed of faith, mold me and help
me to grow; I'm willingly pliant.

So when that seed in me has been nurtured and watered,
I will be forever with You, and that's all that matters.

Hide

Trying to hide the dirt on my hands
By putting them behind my back,

As if He doesn't see or understand
The stains on them and all that I lack.

If I would just come before Him in repentance,
Asking for forgiveness for all I've done,

Then I'd know I have His acceptance
And all my sins would be forgiven; they are a great sum.

Now I don't have to hide anymore.
The weight has been lifted off my shoulders.

Someday I will walk with Him on His celestial shore,
Most likely before I'm very much older.

Just Like You

When? What? Where? How? These are
the questions I'm asking of You.
For that is how I learn what You want me to do.

Give Your Spirit to me when I read Your Word,
To live in me and work in me. Anything else I can't afford.

Guide me and direct me in the direction I should go
So that in my life, Your influence does really show.

When the work is finished and You are all through,
I will be exactly all You want me to be—just like You.

Tread God's Word

What do I mean by treading God's Word?
To walk in His Word, brandishing His sword.

To put into practice all of it, not part,
That we may avoid or disperse Satan's darts.

To bring His joy to all around you,
And to sing His praises daily too.

To show beyond a shadow of a doubt
That you carry His power, His clout,

So that your job performance is sure and true,
That you are His child in everything you do.

The longer I follow His pathway,
The easier it is to always stay.

So, my precious Father, I pray You'll always find my tread,
And I will have nothing whatsoever to dread.

In the World's Eyes

In the world's eyes, I am forty, but in
God's eyes, I am but a babe.
But through His loving, kind, and gentle
care, He is showing me the way.

In the world's eyes, I have come a long way,
but in God's eyes, I have just begun.
They say I have lived half my life, but
in Him, I will never be done.

In the world's eyes, I must struggle alone; but
in God's eyes, His Son is supporting me.
He leads and guides me, disciplines and loves me, and
has set me wonderfully and marvelously free.

In the world's eyes, when I die, I have gone;
I am nothing but dust and bone.
Ah, but in God's eyes, He has led and guided
me and brought me home sweet home!

If You See in Me

If you see in me someone who is faithful, it is not me.
If you see in me someone who is loyal, it is not me.
If you see in me someone who is not a gossip, it is not me.
If you see in me someone who loves one's brother, it is not me.
If you see in me someone who is patient, it is not me.
If you see in me someone who is kind, it is not me.
If you see in me someone who is understanding, it is not me.
If you see in me someone who is spiritual, it is not me.
It is the Spirit of God, the Holy Spirit that lives in me,
Who does and is everything good in me.

God Uses Me

God uses me as a vessel to bring forth light.
And that light is getting stronger and stronger.
Every day and in every way, it lasts longer and longer.

Within me He gave a love so great and a
peace for which I used to hunger.
Why O why did I wait so long; why couldn't I
have found Him when I was younger?

He's given gifts to use for His work, and the
blessings He showers on me you can't count.
And when I run dry, which I do often, there's always
one place I can go—to the One who is my
Fount.

I don't do much in my little corner of the world,
but He has shown me He's pleased as long
As I look to Him for guidance and protection.
He makes me very strong.

Pretty soon you'll see more of Him than
me; yes, you'll see Him, not me.
For you can have this love and peace; you too can be set free.

Just answer when He knocks; just say yes when He calls.
For He gave that freedom once and for all.

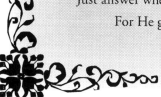

$\mathcal{H}$unger

There are times when I have a deep hunger for God's Word.
There are more now than there used to be.

I'm working toward the time when I'll be just like the Lord
And the Word is burned deep inside of me.

Until that time, and with each day that passes,
I will pray continually for it to happen.

I do not want to be like the masses.
I know He will help me; on that I can depend.

Until that day, I'll continue to fill that hunger
By reading God's Word and delving deeper
into His love, glory, and grace.

He will continue to change in me
selfishness, willfulness, and anger
Until that glorious day I meet Him face-to-face.

I Came to Jesus

You ask me how I gave my heart to Christ; I do not know.
There came a yearning for Him in my soul so long ago.

I found that earth's flowers would fade and die.
I wept for something that would satisfy.

And then, and then, somehow I seemed to dare
To lift my broken heart to God in prayer.

I do not know; I cannot tell you how.
I only know He is my Savior now.

Followership

In this church we have followership.
We have two song leaders who didn't lead,
But they followed where the need led.
Followership—leadership!

We have Sunday school teachers who were pulled into service.
There was a need; they followed.
Followership—leadership!

We have people who do work for the church.
There was a need; they followed.
Followership—leadership!

The pastor of our church wasn't always a pastor.
He was called; he followed.
Followership—leadership!

We are to be great *followers* of Him.
He will make *leaders* of us.
Followership—leadership!

Brother

I just wanted to say thank you for the special person you are,
And while there are more of you, each one my shining star.

By blending and cooperating, we make a very good team.
The Lord has blessed me in my brother, it does seem.

Thank you for each of you doing your individual parts.
You were there right from the start.

So may God bless you, guide you, and keep
you for the rest of this life here,
Knowing that even in heaven, even there you'll be near.

Casting Out

What is it that I will out cast?
Is it something that will last?
Casting out means throwing out,
And giving freely is what it's all about.

I can cast out gossiping and complaining,
Selfishness, greed, and debasing.
Of these I can cast out all, and that is a fact.
And on each new reminder I will act.

And as I go along and I do grow,
I'll add a few as I do go.
And in the end, when I go to the heavenly palace,
I'll be pure and clean without any malice.

And right there beside me will be all the ones who did the same.
To spend my eternity with the one of kingly fame.

$\mathcal{A}$ppreciated

Do I do what I do for me or for the Lord?
Am I doing it for the applause or for God?

I have to search deep inside me and cut deep with the holy sword
To see if it is me or the Holy Spirit they applaud.

Then I realize it is only I who can attest
To the fact that I'm doing right or wrong,
and of course, I must confess.

It's always nice to hear applause, but
the fact remains, it's the best
If it is for God—nothing more, nothing less.

Whether I like the applause or not, it really doesn't matter.
It all belongs to God, you see, and that ends the matter.

Friends

Friends are for sharing, caring, loving, and giving,
To make life brighter and easier just for living.

You are the one I turn to when things go wrong.
You are the one I share with when things run smoothly along.

You are the one I care for, the one I love,
Loving and peaceful as the cooing of a dove.

It's marvelous to share this great life with you.
There's nothing in this world I'd rather do.

The Lord has blessed me with a husband for a friend
And has kept it going till the very end.

But O what a great thing it will be
When in heaven we will share an eternity.

$\mathcal{I}$ Thank You, God

I thank You, God, for the shield You put around
me when I was exposed to a den of sin.
I thank You for Your protection when it was danger I was in.

I thank You for the food You gave, the heat, and the clothes.
For these things were a luxury and were enjoyed; oh yes, I know!

I thank You for the husband You gave, who
has provided for all my needs.
I thank You, Lord, for guiding me where You lead.

I thank You, Lord, for bringing me to Your side.
In You I will always abide.

I thank You, God, for the Son You gave to me,
For without this gift of love, I would never be!

Pray for His People

They didn't choose to be His people.
I weep and pray, always as an example,

That they might know He chose them,
Not the other way around as the thinking has been.

To help them know what an honor it is.
And because of them He has let us in to be His.

So I'll continually pray for Israel as He asked me to do.
That I might do all He asks me to.

Never giving up, never ceasing, always to be pleasing You, Lord,
And encouraging one another that we might be of one accord.

$\mathcal{L}$imited Obedience

He is limited by our obedience.
If we don't obey, how can he help with our existence?

If He tells us what to do and we don't obey,
The good He intended can't be accomplished, come what may.

He is a God who wants us to be in His will.
By using our own will, He then can us fill.

I don't want to limit Him by disobeying.
And always to follow Him is what I'm praying.

Deliver Us

O Lord God, deliver us from the evil one.
Erase the things that we have done.

Throw them as far as the east is from the west
And do for us that which is best.

Keep us from making the same silly mistakes.
Guard us from listening to fakes.

Help us always to walk as Jesus Christ,
And help us to do it at any price.

Help us always to look forward to coming home to You,
Doing the glorious things You do.

Veil of Unbelief

The veil of unbelief is a deadly thing.
It comes in varying degrees, for of pain and death it does bring.

So help my unbelief no matter where it sets.
Turn it into power the kind You have let.

Tear that veil and rip it apart
Like you did at the Crucifixion; at the top You did start.

After You have ripped it apart and the
glory of You shines through,
My unbelief will be gone and there will be nothing You can't do.

All Who Believe

He is the Lord of all who believe,
All who are ready to receive

The wonderful gift of grace,
So freely given without a trace

Of vengeance, cruelty, or injustice,
Freely given to all of us.

Such a simple thing He asks us to do.
Why is it so hard for me and you?

The evidence is all around,
From the sky down to the ground.

O precious Lord, now that I believe,
Let me help others to receive.

ℋis Light in Me

In His—Jesus's—light, the true me shines through.
It hides nothing from You.

Better still, He hides nothing from me,
So He can let me see

The changes that need to be perfected
Of one chosen and elected.

My Lord, always let that special light shine
So that You will always and ever be on my mind.

All May Answer

Keep me shining and faithful
To Your love and grace most wonderful

That the light in me the world may see,
That great faith they might have in Thee.

So shine in me, my everlasting love,
And because of it draw more people to You above,

So that when You come to gather all You have called,
Every one of them will answer—yes, one and all.

$\mathcal{A}$llowed Work of God

What is your response to the calling of God?
What work for Him have you allowed?

I've asked myself that many times,
And the negative answers I've given is a crime.

So many times I should have said yes,
But I let doubt assail my mind instead.

But I promise You, Lord, in the future,
That I will pray and seek for discernment so I'll know for sure

That it's You who sends me on these tasks,
That You are the one who asks.

For All Time

I don't want to be left behind.
I don't want to be *that* certain kind.

I don't want to be left with ties that bind.
Oh, please let me last for all time.

Oh, please don't let me find
That when Jesus came, I was left. *That* I would really mind.

Eternity is a long time to be hell-entwined.
I want to be with Jesus to sup and dine.

So, Lord Jesus, wash away my grime.
I really do want to be with You for all time.

New Body, New Mind

A new body and a new mind.
It sounds impossible, but it's easy, you'll find.

The new mind is brought on by the reading
and accepting of the Word;
The other is brought with the coming of the Lord.

These things are what I have striven for
Ever since I answered the knock on the door.

When I learned of these things,
I wondered why the world wouldn't shout and sing.

What a glorious thing it will be to have
The mind and body that Christ has.

So You Will Know

When God shows His power, He does it for a reason,
Working throughout all seasons,

Saying, "So that you will know that *I am God!*"
Does this not make you feel humbled and awed?

There are no words that can describe
All that He makes me feel inside.

To describe Him is impossible.
My attempts are not even commendable.

So I ask the Holy Spirit to intercede,
Hearing my heart's cry and pleas.

The things I can't put into words or action
For God's own satisfaction.

Everywhere I Go

I want to take You with me everywhere I go.
I want You in everything I see and upon
me Your grace to bestow.

I want to acknowledge You in all that I
do—also in the actions I take.
I will do it all for You and help others to share and partake.

I want only Your glory to show through.
To please You is my goal.
I want the life anew so that I'm not living in the cold.

For I want the world to know how wonderful You
are, and all about Your mercy, grace, and love.
For there are no other gods, either near or far,
that can sit on Your majestic throne above.

At Work Today

The Lord was at work again today,
Allowing me to perform His tasks.

He allowed a woman with me to stay
So that I might give my testimony as He asked.

He allowed someone to see His strength through me.
He allowed someone to give me a helping hand.

He allowed that very someone to see
His glory and grace and to understand.

My prayer to Him is that He continues
to use me in His working grace,
To tell of His wondrous love story,
Until in His time we will meet face-to-face
And I see Him in *all* His glory.

Fill Your Heart

It's hard for me to give solace when you're
deep in the bowels of grief,
To find the right phrases or words that I know will bring relief.

So all I can do is to let you know we care,
And in this thing that hurts so deep we are willing to share.

We will always be there to help you to bear
And to let you know that you are always in our prayers.

I hope this lightens the load just knowing we're your friends.
Upon this absolute fact you can always depend.

So I'll leave this little phrase to fill you heart:
May God bless and keep you, never to depart.

$\mathcal{F}$orgiveness Is a Gift

Forgiveness is a gift. Just watch and do,
And see what glorious riches come to you.

O what relief, what joy, what peace.
When you give everything to Jesus, the aggravation does cease.

Life becomes simpler, more beautiful, and strong.
And within your heart and soul it does put a song.

So come sing it with me this forgiveness stuff,
And stop making life so hard and so rough.

Come sing a song with me full of joy and light.
See what forgiveness can do. Boy, what a great delight!

Foundations

Upon this day a foundation was started.
He came and taught and was an example.

He was tortured and crucified, and then He departed.
But was what He did really so simple?

No! It was not, this deed He had done.
He paid a debt for all who sinned. He for us all was labeled.

He did not do it just for some; He did it
for all who are willing to come.
He gave His life willingly to make us able

To love Him and to follow him in unquestioning loyalty,
From now until forever, throughout eternity.

So celebrate the day the foundation was started.
And be glad that He temporarily departed

Just for a little while. And then His Spirit came back
To guide us and to help us in the things we lack.

$\mathcal{E}$fforts of Mankind

The puny efforts of humans
Only lead to sin.

By looking around you'll find
The light of His glory divine.

The works of many destroy,
While God's love and work bring joy.

The love of humankind, only humankind hinders,
Whereas God's starts a fire from a cinder.

Humankind's self-love is only ever evil,
Whereas God's love through Jesus saves His people.

The choice is yours, given freely,
To be saved and to accept all He is completely.

Earnestly

Earnestly seek Him in your prayer.
Earnestly see Him everywhere.

Earnestly walk in His path.
Earnestly accept His rod and staff.

Earnestly seek Him in times of trouble.
Earnestly clean out all the rubble.

Earnestly do all that you can.
Earnestly by your side He'll stand.

Freedom

Glory, hallelujah, and praise the Lord.
To deny the Son is a price you can't afford.
So offer yourself up to Him
And let Him live within.

Let Him guide and protect you
And save your soul.
Know that He's there for you.
Please make this your goal.

So get down on your knees and pray with me.
Ask Him to come in, and He'll set you free.
He'll give you freedom to show you how to love
With the love from God above;

Freedom from a life of sin
All because of His love within;
Freedom to have eternal life,
Where there will be no more sorrow or strife.

You can have all this and more
Just by asking Him in and opening your heart's door.

Giving Away God's Gifts

Have you tried to give the gift of love away today?
If you have, I'll bet the return was doubled when repaid.

Have you tried giving away His mercy too?
I'll bet He's doubled even that for you.

And what about forgiveness; have you
tried giving that away also?
I'll bet that, like me, you have a ways to go.

Have you given away the gift of prayer?
That's something else we must work on and become a stayer.

There are many more gifts we could give away,
So try to think and give away today.

But there is one gift more important than any.
Today did you give any to Jesus? How many?

Good Thing

The only good thing about me is God.
In the past, if there were a problem, it I would dodge.
I would lie and hide, thinking it would go away,
But it wouldn't; it would only be compounded day by day.
Then there was selfishness in my heart.
I wouldn't do anything unless for me there was a part.
Then there was the temper as black as night,
Losing control at any cost, trying to win the fight.

Then Jesus came into my life
And cut all away as if with a sharp knife,
Replacing the anger with patience and compassion.
Taking away the temper is my admission.
Digging away my selfishness a little at a time,
Replacing it with a love for all mankind.
He put the fear of God in my heart instead of the fear of man.
He did it with grace and love as only He can.

Changes and Saves

God saves you to His good purpose
And changes you, making you whole.

Why else would He send His Son, do you suppose?
And when he changes us, He makes us of more value than gold.

Our lives weren't worth much before,
Just garbage, dirt, and dust.

But now we're purified right down to the core,
Taking away the hard-cased crust

So that we can work for God with purified hearts,
Knowing He gives us the power and strength.

Putting your trust totally in Him is really smart.
To follow Him I'll go to great lengths.

$\mathcal{A}$t Home

Ah, home, where I can relax.
But meanwhile I cannot be lax.

I must do everything the Lord asks while I'm here
To prove Jesus really did appear,

That He really did come to save the world,
And that if we accept Him we're His precious pearls.

Working diligently and hard and fast
As He perfects a crown that lasts

Till the day I get home and have total rest in Him.
To see that day soon is the longing of my heart! *Amen!*

Graceful Growth

The growth He has worked in me
Is something most people won't believe.

In the past, if someone needed a special hug,
I would back off and treat them like a thug.

To even speak to someone brought fear and pain,
And I felt that by it nothing would be gained.

But God's glorious grace came and gave to me
Precious freedom and peace deep down within my being.

If He can do that with such a worm as I,
Can you imagine what He'll do for you?
Believe me, I wouldn't lie.

The Smooth Path

I have not come down the whole road.
Some of it has not been easy because of
my chosen traveling mode.

The burden could have been lighter had
I been willing to turn it over.
Had I given it to Jesus, it would have been better.

Had I run the whole way with Him by my side
And used His way as my only guide,

The road would have been smoother,
all the bumps and hills gone.
For that smooth path, how I did long,

Until I saw the work He did in me
And the creature I used to be.

How the anger, bitterness, and revenge are all left behind,
Replaced by cheer, compassion, and love for mankind.

I've still a long way to go, but I've no
doubt He's all my hope and stay.
Never to go back is what I pray.

The Way Out

I was in the depth of a despair-filled cup
When He took my life and turned it right side up.

When it was upside down and I had nowhere to turn,
It was then of Him I did learn,

How all one needed to do was call on His name.
The people whom He did answer spread His fame

Because of the glory in their lives He did fill,
Which made the talking of Him a big thrill.

So, if you want out of the hole you are in,
Please, come ask Jesus the Savior in.

Holding On

How can I love the unloving?
Lord, You ask too much of me!

But wait, You are there watching,
Waiting for me to call on help from Thee.

Lord, how am I to help this person
When I am unable to help myself?

God, I know You told me to call on Your Son
And use Him and all His wealth.

But most assuredly I am weak,
And I find it hard to grasp Your strength.

Then I relied on the promises of which You speak,
Then hold on at length.

I Trust

I trust in what God can do.
He's ever present and in view.

His love is so great that He sacrificed His Son
To save us from sin and defeated in death, the battle won.

He walks alongside us. We have to know
That letting Him work in us does always show.

What a wonderful, merciful God we have,
Loving us, caring for us, like a balmy salve.

So as I give honor to Him, and glory and praise,
I will be a witness for Him, His banner raise.

Search Me, O God

Search me, O God. How hard it was to ask.
The fear I had about being so open made it a very great task.

It meant that I really wanted Him to know me very intimately,
Even the very bad things, as if He didn't know really.

Then a strange thing happened, a realization of old:
All I needed to do was to come before Him and be bold.

When I ask Him, "Search me, O God," and mean it,
How great and glorious the benefit.

So now you see before you a spirit that is free,
And all I had to ask was, "O God, search me."

The Holy Spirit, Is He in Me?

How can I be free from arthritis, neuritis, and
sciatica without Him? I can't. He healed me.

How can I be free from ulcers and allergies
without Him? I can't. He healed me.

How could I have made it through all the illnesses of
friends and family? I couldn't, not without Him.

How could I have made it past the alcohol and abuse
without any scares to speak of? I could not without Him.

And how could I make it through the trials I'm
going through? I can't, not without Him.

The Holy Spirit, is He in me? You be the judge. Could I have
gone through all that and still have peace? Is He in me? Is He?

What Would I Do without You?

What would I do if You were not here?

How could I make it without You?

How could I survive without You there?

The days would seem barren and endless;

The nights, terrifying and drear.

But I know Your mercy is boundless

And that when I call, You are always near.

So, what would I do without You?

I would fall in the pit so deep,

But mercifully I don't have to.

Always Your promise to me did You keep.

One Among Many

A little girl was born on November 4, 1945.
I wonder, do the parents care if she is alive?

The father was an alcoholic, and the mother not yet.
They are not aware of He who paid their debt.

She was exposed to all sorts of sin as
the parents later ran a tavern.
As danger and trouble did abound, the
angels hovered around her.

As years passed and the parents moved from place to place,
The children were hungry and dirty, with
"dirty white trash" thrown in
Their faces.

With a hunger for love in the girl, deep inside,
It left the door open for tragedy to hide.

But by the grace of God He led her to a boy who cared,
And a human love they did share.

Still there was a hunger for a food she could not
find. Then Jesus came into her heart
With promises that He would never depart.

Now the life is complete, the hunger now known
As something that only Jesus can fill—yes, only He alone.

You Made It Possible

You made it possible to make a clear choice
And made it possible for us to voice

The love and respect that You deserve
As You continue to us preserve.

You made it possible to cleanse us from sin.
You made it possible for our new lives to begin.

You made it possible to spend eternity with You.
You made it possible because You first loved us. Now we can
Love You.

Exploding Darkness

Inner darkness that's hidden from view,
It bubbles and churns as it stews,

Boiling up to explode, devouring everything in sight.
Against such darkness it is hard to fight.

But by the mighty power of the blood of Jesus,
The purifying might cleanses us.

The Holy Spirit that lives within
Guides us away from the direction of sin.

So for their help I thank You, God.
I am humbled and enlightened and stand in awe.

Forever with Us

One of God's many blessings is that He is forever with us.
For some I'm sure that makes them very nervous.

But for me it gives me such peace,
Causing my worry and fear to cease.

It is awesome to know He is with me at every turn
And that He handles whatever waters Satan decides to churn.

What a special blessing to know that every step He guides
As long as in Him I abide.

So always and forever I will give Him His glory and praise
As I stand permanently with the Ancient of Days.

It's All About You

It's all about You, Lord.
Even though You give me rewards,

It's for Your honor, Your glory.
All is about Your Son's story.

It's about all the love that You have for us.
How can we do any less than give You all our trust?

Everything we say and everything we do
Has only to do with Your plans for You.

For You have nothing but good in store,
Nothing but blessings galore.

$\mathcal{G}$arbage

He stood in the garbage heap and pulled me out.
He showed me what He was all about.

How He would cleanse me through and through
And make me all brand new.

How He would be there as I walked His path,
Guiding and protecting me with His rod and staff.

How I could just call out His name,
Ever the comforter through my pain.

No other god could do these things.
I love Him with all my heart, soul, and being.

Who is this God and Savior of whom I speak?
Only Jesus, my Lord, whom everyone seeks.

ℒight Reveals

The Word is light, and it reveals the darkness.
It exposes all my evil and weakness.

I thank the Lord that He provided a way
To take my evil and rid me of it, for the penalty has been paid.

Teaching, admonishing, getting rid of my own will,
And making me listen to His peace: be still.

How marvelous and loving our God is.
To know that the glory can only be His,

To know that we can totally trust in Him,
For we can do nothing for the iniquity we're in.

It is only He who does all the work for us.
Nothing and no one does what He does.

The Burden That's Not a Burden

There is a heavy burden on my heart,
And lifting it is God's part.

It's the souls of my family, friends, and foes.
Praying for them continually is my constant goal.

I hope to lift them for God to see.
I wish them to be a part of Him, deep in the heart of me.

Crying to Him deep within,
I lift my burden to Him,

Knowing that He will respond
And that Him I can depend upon.

Because His will is my will,
And all His promises He does fulfill.

His Works

They are His work and not mine.
He only used my hands.
Through His great power divine
I carry out His commands,

Knowing the work He
Bade me to do.
He has divine purpose behind
To draw, through me, Him to you.
No greater task can I find.

His gifts upon me he does bestow
To use in the works of His kind.
Through me His grace and love flows;
Not an ounce or a whit do I mind.

If the Lord Wills

I've got many plans today,
Things to do, whether to go or stay,

Plans that mount up high.
And sometimes I wonder why.

It is then I say, "If the Lord wills."
And I pray to the Lord and remain still.

I'm running before Him, not knowing where to go,
But I do not question. He then shows.

I'm learning to seek Him first, then go accordingly.
And I find things run smooth with less stress spiritually.

It Takes Time to Get to Perfection

Many years I've been walking the narrow road.
Many a long row needed to be hoed.

Still many more that have to be done
To get to the perfection of the Holy One.

It takes time to get there—
Hard work, sweat, and sometimes despair—

Only because sometimes I lose sight of the Son,
Who would help me get the work done.

But as long as we keep holding on in faith,
The perfection will come at the pearly gates.

My Love for God

How much do I love God?
It's a question that's hard to answer.
I poke, and pry, and prod.
To find out is a great pressure.

My heart is hard to fathom at its best.
How can I know what I don't understand?

I find it hard to be at rest,
So I'll keep searching as hard as I can,

Until my love for Him grows deeper and deeper
And I can state unequivocally,

Without doubt or whisper,
"It will last throughout eternity."

$\mathcal{Y}$ou Called

Before I met You, I had heard of You,
Subtly through whispered words and then songs too.
It was to me unreal the glorious stories they told.
Like a pretty fairy tale they did unfold.
It sounded too good to be true,
The lovely story they told of You.
Then slowly but surely You worked Your way into my life
With words of victorious living and of
helping me through the strife.

First it was just getting to know You
Through the people I talked to.
They told me what You did in their lives and through them,
Of Your wonderful workings—how, where, and when.
Then You started coming to me through Your glorious Word.
In me a thirst You have stirred.
It is so strong in me now that I've accepted Your Son,
And I can't wait for you to complete the work you've begun.

So now, dear Lord, I can see Your face
and hand in everything I do.
It gives me strength and guidance. That helping hand is You.
I thank You for calling my name.
I shall never be the same.
Thank You also for changing in me
The old nature so that like You I may be,
So that I can be Your heir
Till You come and take me in the air.

Persistent

I ask forgiveness for my sin
And promise to try not to do it again.

But I keep falling back into the mire.
And in persistence I will, with Christ's help, those sins retire.

I'll keep fighting it as long as I have breath
Because I want to be like Jesus unto death.

I know He will always help as long as
my heart is right with Him,
Working to perfect me without and within.

Therefore I will always be persistent,
Knowing my God, who is benevolent.

Requirements

My mission is clear, but it's not easy.
Some of the things I have to do are not to me pleasing.

It requires compassion for people I don't like,
And it requires action when I'd rather say, *Go fly a kite*.

It requires study and quiet time
And walking the straight and narrow line.

It requires giving all of myself to Christ,
But it's not near enough for the paid-in-full price.

No, it's not easy being a fanatical Christian,
But it beats being on the other side with Satan.

Revealing Me

What do my words reveal?
What part of me do I not see?

Is it anything to the Lord's appeal?
Do they see I've been set free?

Can they tell I have God's peace? Or that with
Him for His people I mourn and cry?
Can they see that of God's family I'm a
part? Or do they think it is all lies?

Only through Christ can I see the truth,
His revealing to me who I really am.
What people see is the unveiling proof.
If He can change me, He can change you! Yes, He can!

Right Foundation

I'm building on the foundation of Christ,
My life, my home, my all;

Thanking Him for the unspeakable price,
For taking my sin, my fall;

Learning what He has to say
And letting Him guide me on my pathway

So that when the foundation is built and strong,
It will keep me from stepping wrong.

As I build, beyond it, it is true:
Straight and narrow as a witness for You.

When He calls me to work through Him,
The light will be bright, not dim.

Pray They See You

Lord, it is only by Your grace that I'm here.
I'm so glad that You are near.

The things I have gone through in my life,
All the heartache, hunger, danger, and strife,

Have taught me about Your grace and love
And the Holy Spirit's power sent from above.

It is only by this that You have kept me safe
And taught me how to behave.

Your grace and love now shine through.
I pray always that when people look at me, they see You.

Take My Hand

Lord Jesus, take my hand.
Help me do what You command.

Lift me up and help me rise.
Keep me from helping the father of lies.

That You guide me and protect me is my request;
To be exactly like You is my quest.

I give You all praise, glory, and honor.
For now and ever after I'll raise Your banner,

I know You lift me up when I am down.
I have the knowledge that You'll always be around.

Thank You, Lord

Thank you for everything. Whether at work or at play,
I know that through everything by my side You'll stay.

Thank You for the insight You give me
when everything goes wrong
And for being there when I'm helpless, making me strong.

Thank You for the laughter that brightens me along the way.
I get all of You if in return I trust and obey.

Thank You for the friends You've given whom I don't deserve.
I will do my very best to worship and serve.

Thank You, dear Lord, and glory to Your name.
But thank You most of all because I shall never be the same.

That the World My Know

Let my actions be Yours
That the world may know that You are Lord.

Then let them know what is in store
If they don't take up the cross instead of the sword.

Please let my talk reflect Your soul
To make them hunger for Your Word.

To be like You is my goal.
Bind us to You with a very strong cord.

In this way will the world know
That You are the one and only Lord.

Then when You call, they will go,
For they will know that any other decision they can't afford.

Unusual

Lord, help me to be ready always for the
unusual places and unusual things;
To be ready to be of help to the helpless masses of human beings;

To look in the mundane for unusual answers;
And to look in the unusual for the mundane answers.

Help me to be permanently on call for all You ask me to do,
To accept the work without a preview.

Then when the unusual and usual show up,
I'll be ready to handle it without any ifs, ands, or buts.

Words

Let my words, Lord, be as Yours,
That they might bring someone to Your doors.

Let my words never deviate from Your Book.
Please, let me stop, learn, and look.

Put a guard upon my tongue
So that from You others do not run.

From now on and always, make it so that
they can't tell me from You.
O that they might find me doing as You do.

Words That Save

Lord, I ask You to give me words that save,
Keeping others from being a worldly slave.

Make my heart be filled with caring
And my mouth be filled with sharing.

Give me this special love that comes from Your grace
So that they too may see Your glorious face.

Help me to show this with compassion and understanding
So that they will turn to You, not withholding.

*Y*our Blessings

May Your blessings be Your people who lie in obedience,
Who do Your will continually and obey Your
Word with Your Spirit's assistance.

May we never fall short of Your gloriousness
So that of Your love and life we do confess,

So that everything You ask of us
We do without argument, strife, or fuss.

Help us be assured that even though we don't know the plan,
You will still give us a helping hand.

Until the day that we are through,
May we always be a blessing to You.

Battles

One more battle, one more day.
Lord, thank You for helping me all the way,
Guiding and protecting me come what may.
Close beside me is where You promised to stay.

As I get up in the morning and the arrows start flying,
My faith and stamina the devil is definitely trying.

To cope with such things is very hard to do.
Only through Your grace, Lord, do You
help me make it through.

The darts start coming faster as I get to You closer.
He pulls from all directions as the battle gets tougher.

It is now nearing the end, Lord. I wouldn't have missed it at all,
For You are closer to filling my whole
being, guarding me from a fall.
Sometimes I've done what I shouldn't have,
but most times I do what I ought.
Through You I've won the victory, won the battles I have fought.

The Father

I can think of no other way than to send My people a sacrifice.
I will have to send My Son so that for them He will give His life.

They will not listen, so there's no other way
To save My people so they can come home to stay.

I must send Him down to go through this terrible ordeal,
To take the sins of mankind, their troubles
and depressions, and to heal.

Go now, My Son, for this special task I send You to do.
I know You will be obedient, honest, and true.

I see Him now doing the work for which I sent Him,
Teaching love and kindness, making ears to hear
and healing eyes that have gone dim.

But the hour approaches that I find hard to bear,
For I love Him and am pleased with
Him, but in this I cannot share.

He is mocked and mimicked and bound and trussed.
They slapped Him, and Him they did cuss.

With stripes on His back and a crown of thorns on His head,
He went up the mount with His cross. They led.

They nailed Him to the cross, and I was with Him to this point,
But now He must take the sins of mankind.
I know He won't disappoint.
O My dear Son, I wish I could be with You
in this, the hour of Your need,
But I can't look on sin, My Son. This You must concede.

The work is now done. "It is finished," He said.
He gave up the ghost, and they pierced His side—and it bled.

The day was dark and cloudy and cold,
But He finished His work; for humanity's sins He atoned.

God was angry and brokenhearted because
of the pain that His Son did bear.
But the first covenant was broken, and the
tabernacle curtain he did tear.

And on the third morning, what a bright and glorious day,
For Jesus had risen, and the price He did pay.

He will now be with Me forever. By My side He will stay.
For now My people can come home if
they but believe in Him always.

$\mathcal{H}$e Carried the Cross

He carried the cross for me upon Calvary hill.
He carried the cross for me. Hanging there
are my own self, pride, and will.

This is the day to remember that all these
things for me He took away.
That I will eternally be in His will—this I pray.

To always remember the agony He went
through as He took away my sin,
That He might as I answered His call be able to call me friend.

I really want to understand someday how
deep this relationship goes.
I want to know Him as he knows me,
from my head down to my toes.

Now I praise His holy name upon this Easter morn
For the body that was beaten, battered, and torn.

Because I know He rose again for all those who will see
That we might be with Him eternally—yes, you and me.

The Curse That Was a Blessing

He hung cursed upon a tree,
This man who came from Galilee.

Bloodied, beaten, humiliated, and scorned,
And pieces of His flesh from His body were torn.

As He hung dying on the cross for all to see,
He said, "Come live in paradise today with Me."

Little did we know or understand
That He was dying for us, this God-Man.

Then came the day of His resurrection,
Thus completing our perfection.

Now we know that His curse became a blessing.
The acknowledgment of this is what we're addressing.

ℐ Birthday Gift

Trials and tribulations. He's in despair.
His troubles cannot be compared.

The man hanging on the cross,
From the depths of hell He has been tossed.

From death He has won the victory.
He did this for you and for me.

Come one, come all, to my precious Lord's side.
In Him truly abide.

For no greater gift can be given for Christ's birth
Than to give Him your soul while you're here on earth.

Today I'll Be with Him in Paradise

As I'm hanging on the cross,
I'm vaguely aware of who He is.

Names of profanity at Him they toss.
Nailing Him to a cross and gambling for
the garments that were His.

I heard my partner in crime reviling Him,
Saying, "Why don't You save yourself if You are this Christ?"

As I felt the agony and pain I was in,
I realized that He now was paying the price.

I asked my friend if he wasn't afraid of God.
Blasphemy was something He couldn't abide.

I asked if He would think of me in His
Kingdom, if He wouldn't think it odd.

I'll never forget the miraculous answer:
"Today you'll be with Me in paradise."

Eternally Pure

I am no innocent. Blood and pain is on my hands.
Beating and humiliation was brought by my command.

A crown of thorns upon His head, and spittle upon His face.
There is no doubt I caused these acts to take place.

Nails pierced His hands as He hung on the cross.
And when He died, into the tomb He was tossed.

Down into the pits He walked, and then rose on the third day.
All this for my degradation, He went willingly to pay.

Now with His loving sacrifice, He has paid for my sin.
He cleansed me and made me pure. I am
eternally His, without and within.

$\mathcal{D}$ress for God

Have you dressed for God today
And put on love, the breastplate?

Have you dressed for God, you elders and youth?
Have you put on the helmet of salvation?

And have you dressed for God even before you pray?
Have you put on your shield of faith?

Ah, and have you dressed for God and in the very
least put on your shoes (the gospel of peace)?

And have you dressed for God today to
keep yourself out of trouble?
Have you put on your sword today—the sword that is the Bible?

1 Thessalonians 5:8; Ephesians 6:14–17

*Y*ou Are the One

You are the one who guides us,
And You are the only one we can trust.

You are the only one who keeps us safe.
We only want to walk in Your way.

You are the only one who give us peace
By giving to us Your love to release.

Just by looking into Your wonderful face,
We see delivered to us Your glorious grace.

You are the only one who saves our souls.
Following You only will be my goal.

You are the only one who does it by grace.
No payment He asks, no, not even a trace.

No Life Before You, Lord

I am turning my life over to you, Lord,
Trying to leave nothing behind.

Reading Your Word daily, in me to be stored,
Taking away the scales that were making me blind.

Removing the stops from my ears—
That is a task I'm looking forward to—

So that everything I hear
Is from Your Word and all brand new.

The only thing left is my heart of stone.
And You are crumbling that day by day.

I know that I'm not walking alone
And that You're holding my hand and
You are with me all the way.

With You, those ever-present misconceptions are not a fear,
Because You are always reliant and wipe away all tears.

My Crown Is Jesus

He is my righteousness,
And I must confess,

He is any glory I might have.
Through Him, on me, His rejoicing He does lath.

He is my incorruptibility,
But more than this, He gives me life eternally.

At His feet I will toss these crowns of many
When I meet Him, because they are His aplenty.

Purchased of God

They say the value of things is the amount that's paid.
If that is the case, then we're worth a vast amount,
Because the ransom that God made
Is beyond measure or count.

How can you put a value on the life of a Son
Or the amount of suffering He had to go through?
It just can't be done,
Yet He did it for me and you.

So if He values me so much,
How can I refuse?
I give Him everything I have as such,
Because I just can't lose.

With His Son's blood, He purchased me.
With my heart I give my life to Him.
With mercy He waits to see
Whether I will choose hell or heaven.

$\mathcal{B}$ecause of God

My heart is beating because of God's will.
Every breath I take is due to Him.

My life and spirit He does fulfill
From my soul and heart deep within.

Everything I am, He makes of me,
Through His Word, trials, and His people,

So that people might look and see
That in God's eye I am His apple.

Through my life and words they see
That they can have the same thing,

That they can also like this be
And to God other people bring.

$\mathcal{I}$ Choose to Love God

I choose to love God always,
No wavering come what may.

I choose to be obedient in all He has me do
As I walk this life through.

I choose to worship Him always with everything I have,
As He protects me with His rod and staff.

I choose to praise His name
As it's always and ever the same.

I choose to honor Him with body, mind, and soul.
This ever is always my goal.

Respect and Awe

Lord God, I stand in great fear of You,
In fear that I will displease You, as surely I will,

Although I try to be obedient in everything I do
And every command fulfill.

I have nothing but reverence and respect.
And I stand in humility and awe.

You never let me go my own way, standing ready to correct,
Never ready to let me fall.

Lord, there never was, nor will there ever be, anyone like You.
And I'll never forget You are holding my hand.

You always cleanse me every day, making me brand new.
Forever I will take Your stand.

The Lord of the Impossible

I do the impossible every day
Through Jesus Christ, my hope and stay.

I get through schedules that can't be done.
And even though I'm on the run,

I get through everything on time—
And even get a break, I find.

My Jesus the Christ is reliable
And is the Lord of the impossible.

Through His power and might,
There's nothing I can't do with Him in sight.

The Remnant

As you read through the Bible, you find
that there is always left a remnant.
That's what I want to be, living in the expectant.

I want to be among the very faithful,
Although life is hard and hurtful.

Because the rewards are more than worth it in the end.
On His help through it all you can depend.

But more than that, the close relationship is beyond price.
It lasts through an eternity with Christ.

What more can one possibly want or need
Than to be with Christ indeed?

Works of the Devil

The works of the devil are destroyed by God.
But first I must give myself to Him.

Because in myself I am flawed,
The flaws rooted deep down within.

But by His grace, He sent His Son
To cleanse and purify.

The battles I must fight are already won,
That His name I might glorify.

It's so hard to admit I'm as depraved as they,
But until I do, I'm walking in pride.

Only by the price He paid
Can I in salvation hide.

Glad in Death

There is a death I am oh so glad for.
And as it slowly dies, I'm glad all the more.

It is the death of my old nature,
And when it goes it will give me great pleasure.

As I am sure the Lord is rejoicing
And that the angels their praises are voicing.

For I know when it is gone,
I'll be in heaven, and for that I long.

God Is a Choice

I have the choice to choose which side I'm on,
Whether Satan's or Jesus's, the Holy One.

I have the choice to be good or bad,
Or even to be happy or sad.

Each has a reflection: either of God in me
Or of Satan and the world's to be.

Whether to be loving and compassionate
Or mean and hateful and from God separate.

The choice was easy to make,
But the walk difficult to take

Till I turned everything over to Him
And let Him work within.

The path is still hard, but I'm not alone.
He helps with my burden, Christ the Cornerstone.

Salesman for God

There are people who can sell anything.
I don't have the ability to sell a life jacket to a drowning man,

But I must learn to sell the most important thing I can bring.
It's the very thing on which others' very souls depend and stand.

Telling them of Jesus and the price He paid,
That He's the only way—I need to help them understand.

Only through the Holy Spirit can I do this.
As His salvation they don't want to miss.

The Trumpet Call

Where will I be when the trumpet calls?
Will I be ready, or will I be with the world when it falls?

Will I be standing on the rooftop, ever alert,
Sounding the warning, the death of souls trying to avert?

Will I be trying to prepare my family and friends?
We must be ready for the coming of the end.

Listening, caring what the Lord has for me to do?
Compassionate and loving, wanting it for you?

I will sacrifice all that I have to give
And what life You give to me. For You I will live!

You Work in Me

Lord God, I want to be right with You,
And so often it is what I fail to do.

You are faithful in sending the Holy Spirit
To tell me when I get out of line. If only I would hear it.

Make me willing to make the changes in my life.
No matter what it takes, cut it out with a sharp knife.

As You work on me, I will give You all the credit,
Because as anyone can see, only You could do it.

When You finally take me home,
I will be perfected when kneeling at Your throne.

Know You Enough

Lord, I don't know You enough! is the cry of my heart.
But the hunger to know You better has
been there right from the start.

The minute I accepted Jesus as my Savior,
You ingrained it even into my behavior.

You have kept me committed and true
And longing to be just like You.

You cleanse me and purify me every day,
Guiding, teaching, and protecting me even as I pray.

But the longing will stop, this I know,
When I get to heaven and holy garments on me You bestow.

For then I'll be as close as I can be,
Praising and bowing on bended knee.

Instead of God

Some people rely on themselves instead of God,
And some people down others' paths have trod.

Some people rely on the sun, moon, and stars.
And some people think that witches
and psychics are better by far.

Some people rely on things and think they're doing well.
But I have God's truth to tell:

How He sent His Son to die for our sins,
And how He invites you to come live with Him.

He gives you the freedom of choice.
All you have to do is your acceptance voice.

$\mathcal{H}$is Right Hand

It's bigger than me, this job I have to do.
His giving me this assignment, who really knew

That God would entrust in me
The work He wants me to see?

Finding if He can depend
Upon me to the very end.

Stretching me, pulling me, putting trials in my life
To show that I am His loving wife,

That I obey His every command
And follow in the likeness of the one at His right hand.

$\mathcal{H}$e's the Only Way

Don't slap God in the face by your unbelief
And then expect Him from your troubles to give you relief.

Don't count on Him always being there if you
continually turn your back on Him.
For it is only through your believing that these things stem.

Don't think that just because you are good, you will be saved.
God says that Jesus is the only true way.

Or that just because you know someone, that will get you in.
Only on a personal relationship with
Jesus can your hopes be pinned.

Just in case you've not gotten what I'm trying to say,
Salvation is through Jesus. He's the only way!

Help

Father, I'm so tired, exhausted, and worn,
And my heart is wrenched and torn.

With every tear and cry she makes,
It's just more than my heart can take.

But always, Lord, I have Your assurance
That You won't crush me in abundance

But will help me grow strong in the trial You gave,
As You've taught me how to walk in Your way.

To rely on Jesus and His power,
Hanging on to His hand every minute, every hour.

You will get me through this test
As I walk in obedience and confess

That I cannot do it without You near.
And the more I talk to You, the more I feel You're near.

So, by Your grace I turn to You.
There's nothing more I need to do.

Printed in the United States
By Bookmasters